将此书献给：

林奥凯 . Antoine & The Moussali 家族 .

特别鸣谢：

著名阳明学专家吴光教授 . 复旦大学中文系祝克懿教授 . Luke Sheehan. 袁冰 . 张韶芹 . 霍智伟 .
崔伽伦 . 蒋心宇 . Grace Ng. Jessica & The Pappalardo 家族 . 张贵东 .

This Book is dedicated to:

Aokai LIN. Antoine & The Moussali Family.

Special Thanks to:

Wu Guang, Wang Yangming philosophies expert. Zhu Keyi, Department of Chinese Language, Fudan University.

Luke Sheehan.Bing Yuan. William Chang. Huo Zhiwei. Gaon Choi. Carol Jiang.

Grace Ng. Jessica & The Pappalardo Family. Zhang Guidong

HELLO Wang Yangming
你好！王阳明

[美]李玉琼 绘　李谷鸣　[美]李玉琼 著
By Kelly Li, Catiah Li

红旗出版社

序

普及王阳明心学的一种有益尝试

顾 久

这是两个既有中国文化情怀，又有西方文化背景的青年女性为中外孩子们写、绘的一本书，用中英文对照着，讲述着中国明代思想家王阳明先生的故事。

坦率说，王阳明心学很难用浅易的文字让人明白，特别是让孩子们明白。为什么？“明白”这个词其实包含两个不太一样的内容：一是从概念上来“理解”，二是从生命经历来“体验”。比如，听到“你获奖了”，弄清楚所说的“你”是谁，“获”了什么“奖”之类，就是“理解”。但你如果从来没有获奖或者失去奖的经验，你就很难从心灵上体会获得或失去奖励的感受，这就是“体验”。既弄清了概念，又有了亲身体验，才能真正“明白”一个人或一个道理。

两位青年作者很认真地思考着中华文化背景中的王阳明及其与西方文化的关系。她们决定用一个个生动而简短的故事，串联起王阳明的一生，以此降低阅读的难度，增加对孩子们的亲和力；她们用视觉引发少儿的兴趣，让抽象的道理与具体的形象之间沟通起来，在已成往古的王阳明与当下孩子们面对生活时的自由选择之间建起一座桥梁……

说真的，我已经习惯了古书和学者中那个学术的王阳明，这样的心学传播方式让我耳目一新。我相信这是一次有意义的尝试。因此真诚地希望两位作者的努力能让国内外的孩子们知道王阳明这个人，并通过文字，理解“心学”；通过故事，感悟中华传统优秀文化；更希望有志的孩子乃至成人能通过本书，体会阳明、体认心学，最后，以他们自己的生命来体会并努力成为一个心中有理想、有坚守、有宇宙、有美感、有崇高的大写的“人”。

（作者为贵州省人大常委会副主任，贵州省文联主席、省文史研究馆馆长）

Preface

A Practical Attempt to Popularize Wang Yangming's Philosophies.

By Gu Jiu

This book is about the story of Wang Yangming (1472-1529), one of the greatest thinkers in Chinese history. It is designed and illustrated by two young cultured women who have backgrounds in both Eastern and Western societies. This bilingual book provides a chance for young people both at home and abroad to gain a glimpse into the renowned philosopher's wisdom.

Wang Yangming's philosophies can often seem difficult to understand. Why do people, especially young people, generally have difficulty grasping his teachings? Well, the word "understanding" actually can be understood in two ways; one is an intellectual form of understanding, and the other is an experiential form of understanding. Perhaps young people lack the experiential part of life that can only be gained through living more life.

For example, if someone were to say, "You won a prize", it could be understood in concept.

However, if one has never won or lost a prize, it would be challenging for them to understand the real meaning of winning a prize. If one has had the experience of winning or losing, then one can fully grasp the true meaning of that statement: "You won a prize." -The experiential knowing with the conceptual knowing creates a full understanding of the event itself.

These two young authors are creating a bridge for modern readers to understand the profound Eastern philosophies of ancient times. Instead of confusing readers with language in classical Chinese prose, they have created an illustrated readable book in multi-languages. Wang Yangming's stories and philosophies can now become accessible to everyone. Also, the styles of the illustrations are original and intriguing to help facilitate one's understanding. This unique piece of work will make it possible to connect modern people with the Chinese notables of ancient times.

Having been accustomed to the academic writings about Wang Yangming, I was quite impressed at first glance. It is hard to imagine that a text full of profound insights can be presented with such eloquent simplicity. I have to say this is an important book; I sincerely hope that the efforts of these two young authors can make Wang Yangming known by more people from around the world. I also hope this book can inspire more modern-day humans to apply ancient Chinese pearls of wisdom.

Wang Yangming's unshakable faith in the human heart and its potential for goodness can inspire an entire universe. I believe Wang Yangming's teachings will be essential for many generations to come.

(*Gu Jiu, the Chairman of the Guizhou Provincial Federation of Literary and Arts, Director of the Provincial Literature and History Research Institute*)

1472 年，一个神奇的梦。

一位母亲怀孕 14 个月后产下一子。在生产之前，她的婆婆做了一个神奇的梦，梦到一位神仙驾着彩云送来一位幼儿。家人觉得这男孩非同寻常，定是上天所赐，于是家中长者给他起名“王云”，并将孩子出生的楼命名为“瑞云楼”。

1472— A Woman Carrying a 14-month-old Baby Gave Birth.

The grandma of the noble Wang family had dreamt of a light spirit ascending to earth in the form of a baby. When she woke up, she knew her grandson was a gift from the heavens. “Wang Yun,” was to be his name as “Yun” meant clouds. The family renamed the building he was born in as the “Rui Yun Building” to match his name.

5 岁，还不开口说话。

王云是个善于观察的小男孩，可就是不说话，长辈都非常担忧。后经一位高僧指点，家人将王云的名字改为王守仁。有一天，他的爷爷正在练习书法，边练边摇着头说：“大学之道……”没想到，就在这时，小男孩接过爷爷的话，把后面的内容全背出来了。大家都十分惊讶。

The 5-year-old Mute Finally Spoke.

Wang Yun was a quiet, observant little boy for years. Everyone around him was worried as he was not a willing talker. Under the directions of a senior monk, the family decided to change his name to Wang Shouren, believing that the change will get him to speak. One day, his grandfather was writing calligraphy in his study. He had a habit of reciting aloud the Great Learning by Confucius as he wrote them down. Amidst his practice, as he recited, a little voice behind him finished the remaining prose aloud. Everyone in the house was astonished, and this was the first time the boy had ever spoken a word. Wang Shouren was not a mute, after all.

11 岁，一鸣惊人。

王守仁随祖父上京求学，途中正逢一帮文人墨客在月下饮酒作诗。王守仁兴致勃勃地加入其中。没想到，这个 11 岁的小孩一鸣惊人，在座的大人们都竖起了大拇指。但其中一位长者不太相信他这么小年纪能写出那样的好诗，便令他再写一首关于月亮和山的诗。然而，男孩只想了几分钟，一首富有哲理的诗脱口而出：“山近月远觉月小，便道此山大于月。若人有眼大如天，还见山小月更阔。”

The Eleven-year-old Genius Wrote His First Poem.

Wang Shouren followed his grandfather to Beijing for the start of his formal education. Along the way, they stumbled upon a group of intellectuals drinking and flexing their literary muscles under the moonlight. The boy became intrigued and was excited by the prose he heard. He immediately added lines on the spot by which all the poets were amazed. However, one of the poets did not believe a boy of his age could create anything meaningful in such short notice; his grandfather must have written them. He asked Wang Shouren to compose a poem on the spot with the subject of the moon and the mountain. Wang Shouren pondered for a few minutes, and then officially wrote his very first poem:

“Look, the mountain is standing closer than the moon. Some may say the mountain is a giant. If one’s horizons were as far as the universe, one would see the lofty mountain dwarfed by the giant moon.”

圣

圣人之问。

父亲为王守仁请来一位书塾。有一天，王守仁突然问道：“请教老师，人生中最重要的事情是什么呢？”老师对这位学生感到诧异，瞪着眼睛回答说：“当然是努力学习！如能通过科举考试做官，将前途无量。”男孩想了想，疑惑着小声说道：“也许人生最重要的事是读书学圣贤。”

A Curiosity for Enlightenment Began.

During the Ming dynasty, Beijing was a place of rigorous school systems and talented masters. Masters gave lectures but never engaged their pupils in any form of discussion. One day, Wang Shouren asked, “What is the most important thing in life?” The old master was surprised by the question and replied, “Studying hard is certainly the most important thing in your life. If you are diligent enough to pass the imperial examination, you will have a promising future.” Unsatisfied with the master’s reply, Wang Shouren continued asking, “Maybe, the most important thing is to be enlightened?”

13 岁，第一次面对生死离别。

13 岁那年，王守仁亲爱的妈妈去世了。失去母亲让他十分伤痛。他的父亲又娶了一位夫人，可这位继母对他并不友善。男孩进入了少年时代，他和所有的青少年一样，开始探索世界，也开始学会叛逆了。

First Experience with Death.

When Wang Shouren turned 13 years old, his beloved mother passed away. He could not help but feel a deep sense of loss at his mother’s passing. His father soon remarried a wicked woman, who cared very little for her new stepson. As nature intended, the teenage boy started to explore the world and began to show his rebellious tendencies.

一个小把戏。

有一天，他跟迷信的继母玩了一个小把戏。他在市集上买了一只怪鸟。随后，他收买了一名神婆，请求她与自己配合演一出好戏。男孩回到家后，把怪鸟藏在他继母的床上。继母晚上进入房间时，被突如其来的怪鸟给吓坏了。她随即请来了神婆驱魔。这位和王守仁串通好的神婆假装被男孩的生母灵魂附体，令这位继母噩梦不断。最后继母承诺只要她活着，一定会善待男孩。

Wang Shouren, the Trickster.

One day, he decided to play a trick on his superstitious stepmother. He bought a strange bird from the marketplace. He then convinced a witch to help him and paid her handsomely to enact an episode of spiritual possession.

When he returned home, he hid the bird in his stepmother's bed, and when it came time for bed, his stepmother pushed back the quilts, and to her horror, the bird fluttered out wildly into the room. She immediately sought the town's witch to ward off any evil spirits that may have entered the house.

The witch, as instructed, played her part of being possessed by the ghost of his deceased mother. Nightmares plagued the poor woman for days, and she finally promised the Gods to treat the boy like her own from thereon.

17 岁， 奉命成婚。

古时，年轻人须遵父母之命、媒妁之言成婚。在王守仁小的时候，父亲王华就与一位时任朝廷大员的朋友给儿子定下了婚约，如今王守仁年满 17 岁，便履行其父之命成婚。

Age 17, Marriage, a Step into Adulthood.

Arranged marriages were a common practice in ancient China. Wang Shouren’s father, Wang Hua, had betrothed his son to a high-ranking family. His wife-to-be was the daughter of a court official. In 1488, at the ripe age of 17, it was time for Wang Shouren to become a married man.

喜

失踪的新郎。

新婚当晚，新郎官溜出来散步，没想到这一走就到了一座道观前，道观中坐着一位气定神闲的道士。道士看了一眼新郎官，语重心长地说：“你生病了。”王守仁心中惊了一下，回答说：“我身体确有不适之处，这该如何是好？”

The Missing Groom on a Righteous Path.

The wedding day was glorious. However, right after the ceremony, the groom was nowhere to be found. Wang Shouren escaped all the wedding festivities to go for a walk. He came across a Taoist temple and found a senior Taoist meditating peacefully inside. When he approached the old man, the Taoist glanced at him and said, “From your complexion, I can tell you are not very healthy.” Wang Shouren was surprised and agreed, then responded, “You are right. What can I do about it?”

养生之道。

时空仿佛霎时消失了，两人彻夜谈论养生之道。于是新郎彻夜未归，新娘一人独守婚房。而新郎对他面前这位年岁已高的长辈不知不觉心生敬畏。

Learning the Art of Longevity.

Intrigued by the old man, the young groom continued to probe into his knowledge. The two discussed extensively and covered topics from health preservation to the art of longevity. The conversation was so engaging that Wang Shouren had forgotten to return to his wedding party, leaving his bride all alone until morning. He thought it odd that these words would come from such an aged Taoist, but remained hopeful.

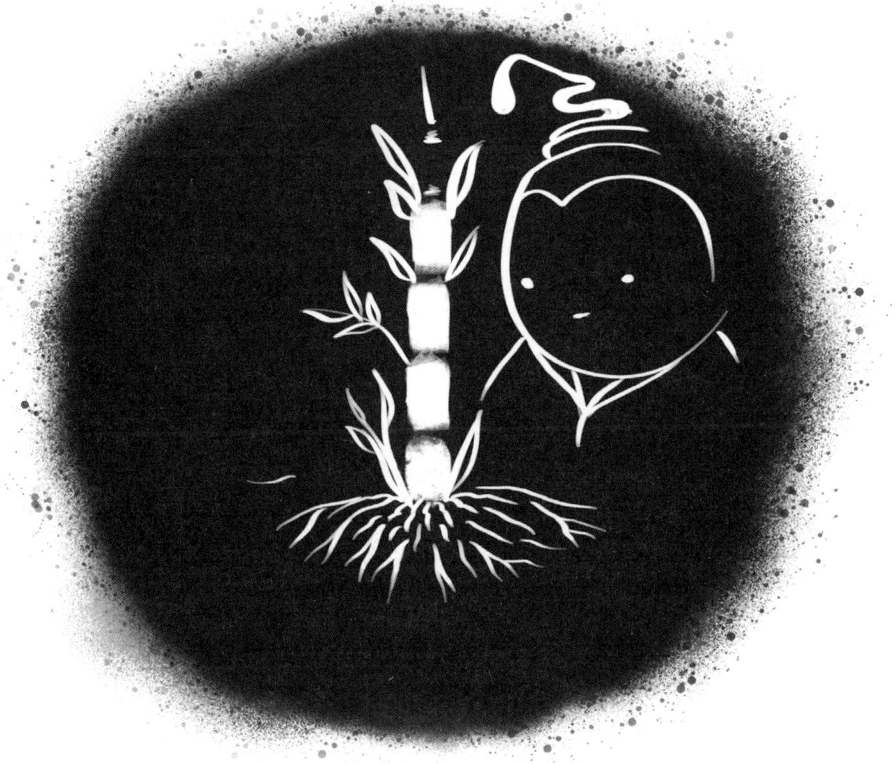

观察竹子。

王守仁一直在追求做圣人。他博览群书，饱读儒家经典，尤其是朱熹的理学。朱熹曾教导过世人：要理解生命的本质，就必须深刻地观察一件事物后悟出个“理”来，达到格物致知。在得到导师娄谅的建议后，王守仁便想通过观察竹子来探索竹子的“理”。

The Bamboo Meditation.

Wang Shouren persisted in pursuing a path in enlightenment. Under the guidance of a mentor, Lou Liang, he began to study the works of Zhu Xi, a reputable philosopher of Neo-Confucianism. Zhu Xi's teachings were called Li Xue, which taught people to observe natural objects thoroughly and intensively to uncover the truth of the universe. Wang Shouren followed the teachings and chose bamboo as the object of observation.

7 天后病倒了。

他还带上一位朋友，和他一起在祖父的后院里“格竹”。但 3 天后他的朋友放弃了。到了第 7 天，他自己也感到烦闷、空虚，最后病倒了。之后，他便认为格物这招不管用，于是开始质疑朱熹的理学。

Empty Lessons.

Sitting and observing bamboo for seven days was no easy task. Wang Shouren invited along a friend to explore the laws of bamboo in his grandfather’s backyard. After three days, bored out of their minds, his friend gave up first. Wang Shouren continued, and after seven days of sitting, thinking, and observing nothing but bamboos, he became depressed and physically ill. He decided that his practice was altogether a waste of time and started to question the concepts of Zhu Xi’s Li Xue.

22 岁，第一次落榜。

科举是当时每个读书人生命中最重要的事，这是决定整个人乃至整个家族兴衰成败的转折点。通过考试的人可以在朝廷中封个一官半职，日后再加官晋爵。21 岁时，王守仁第一次参加浙江乡试，很轻松地就中了举人。然而，第二年春，早已熟读四书五经、满腹经纶且胸有成竹的王守仁却在会试中意外落榜了。

First Failure, Age 22.

The Imperial civil examination system determined the prospects of one's career and even the status of one's family at the time. The examination was designed to test one's understanding of Confucian Classics. Most people who passed could eventually become high ranking officials of the imperial court.

In 1492, 21-year-old Wang Shouren started the examination journey and had passed Xiangshi, the provincial examination with flying colors, which earned him the status of a Juren. Jurens were successful candidates who could then go on to Huishi, the final round of Imperial testing. Overconfident, he thought he could pass the Huishi easily. However, when the test results came out, he failed.

第二次落榜。

第二次参加会试的王守仁又落榜了。其他落榜的考生们悲痛万分，看到此景，他由衷感慨道：“世以不得第为耻，吾以不得第动心为耻。”

Second failure.

His second attempt to pass Huishi also failed. Unlike his peers who were demotivated by their test results, he didn’t think much of it. “It’s not a shame to fail, but it is a shame to see how others are so affected by their sense of shame.” he thought.

创建龙泉诗社。

回到家乡后，王守仁创建了龙泉诗社，吸引了不少文人雅士在此切磋文学。可他依然不忘“做圣贤”的理想，于是诗社不久就解散了。

Enlightenment is to be Sought Alone.

Wang Shouren had more time on his hands after failing his Imperial exams. To further his philosophical studies and be with likeminded individuals, he decided it was best to start a poetry club. He called it “Longquan,” the Dragon Spring Poetry Society. Suddenly he found himself surrounded by philosophers, poets, and other intellectuals. However, not long after its conception, the club disbanded as it took up too much of his time, and he refocused his energies into his enlightenment studies.

26 岁，钻研兵法。

王守仁决定把注意力放在兵法研究上。他钻研战争策略，还成了一名出色的弓箭手。他经常自己制定战术并给士兵们讲解。他还梦见了威宁伯王越。梦中王越将军把自己的弓箭赐予他，祝福他战无不胜。

Learning the Art of War, Age 26.

In spite of his examination failures, Wang Shouren busied himself learning military strategies and the art of archery. He excelled at the courses and even created new unique war tactics for foot soldiers. He was so obsessed with combat strategies that he often dreamt of conversing with his idol, Wang Yue, an eminent general from the Ming Dynasty (1368-1644). In his reoccurring dreams, Wang Yue had given him his victorious bow and blessed him with epic victories.

理

28 岁，第三次会试。

王守仁对人生存在的价值充满好奇。他想更加深刻地理解物质世界是如何与人的内心世界产生连接的。他决定再次深入研究朱熹的理学，并第三次参加了会试。

A Deeper Look into Confucian Classics, Age 28.

Wang Shouren's curiosity about the meaning of life continued to grow as he reached adulthood. He questioned the relationship between one's outer world versus the inner world. To gain a deeper understanding, he had to revisit Zhu Xi's Li Xue concepts from the Confucian Classics and attended Huishi for the third time.

二甲第七

中了进士。

王守仁终于通过了会试，并在殿试中赐进士出身，在当时可是全国第十名。可就算如此，他仍旧没有解开心中的困惑：生命的意义何在？

First Win. Passing the Imperial Exams with Flying Colors.

Finally, Wang Shouren, on his third try, passed the Huishi. He had earned the prestigious title of Jinshi and ranked tenth amongst all the candidates from across the nation. However, even with all his academic success and achievements, he did not feel any more enlightened.

初入仕途。

朝廷安排王守仁在工部任职，他的第一个差事就是修建王越将军的墓，这正是曾在王守仁梦中出现的大将军威宁伯。聪明的王守仁把他之前研习的兵法运用在造墓工程中。在闲暇之时，还把民工们召集起来，训练他们如何作战。一些训练有素的工匠还组成了精英部队。陵墓修建完成后，王越将军的儿子十分满意，最终将父亲生前所佩的宝剑赠予王守仁。王守仁梦想成真，喜不自胜。

The Start of a New Career.

As Jinshi, Wang Shouren took up his first appointment in the Ministry of Works as a construction supervisor. He was to facilitate the renovations of a celebrated general's tomb. Coincidentally, the occupant of the monument was Wang Yue, his childhood idol from his reoccurring dreams. It was during the construction that his military prowess began to become noticed by his superiors. He applied many of his innovative strategies to the project and spent much time training the construction workers on-site during breaks for combat. Eventually, some of his well-trained construction workers joined the Imperial elite forces. The project was a success, and Wang Yue's family was so pleased with the monument that they gifted him the general's sword relic in gratitude.

依然困惑。

即使在职业生涯中取得了成功，王守仁对人生的幸福、存在价值和志向等问题仍无法得出满意的答案。他想既然无法从理学中寻找答案，继续深入研究佛教或道教也许能解答一二。

Perplexed by Life's Complexities and Meanings.

Even with all the new success in his career, Wang Shouren still pondered about happiness and continued to search for the meaning of life. It seemed unlikely that his studies in Li Xue could provide any satisfactory answers. So, he started digging into Buddhism and Taoism.

对儒学产生兴趣。

山中冥想似乎通常是一个悟道的好方法。王守仁在九华山寻到一位道士，老道指点他多钻研儒学最上乘的修行方法。他对王守仁说："周濂溪（周敦颐）和程明道（程颢）是儒家的两个好秀才。"王守仁深深地被这位老道的观点所吸引。第二天一大早，王守仁想再次请教老道，可惜老道已不在洞中。他有些失望。

Searching for the Roots of Confucianism.

Many believed that to reach high levels of enlightenment, one had to meditate deeply in seclusion, and mountain caves were the preferred place for those seeking profound solitude. Wang Shouren found an old Taoist priest in the Jiuhua Mountains who advised him to look into Zhou Lianxi and Cheng Mingdao - the two pioneers of Neo-Confucianism who were known qualified disciples of Confucius himself. Wang Shouren felt grateful to have some direction. The next day, he returned to the meditation cave of the old priest in hopes of learning more. However, the cave was deserted, which left many unanswered questions for the curious student.

31 岁，预感灵验。

在九华山中没有“悟道”的王守仁，又决定去老家会稽山学习导引术。据说这是一种古老而神秘的养生术，修之可长生不老。他在此修行、调养生息。有一天，他让他的学生去山下接访客。弟子将信将疑，没想到果真有人来访。众人惊愕，以为王守仁快要得道升仙了。

Learning the Art of Prophecy, Age 31.

It was difficult for Wang Shouren to find the root authors of Confucianism, and after some time, he gave up on the task altogether. He returned home and continued to meditate in a nearby cave in the Kuaiji Mountains. There, he stumbled upon a new practice called Daoyinshu, an ancient and mysterious practice that allowed individuals to have acute visions for the future. Wang Shouren became immersed in the practice, and one day, he suddenly foresaw a visit from a stranger. He immediately dispatched one of his pupils to the foot of the mountain and instructed them to wait for the unknown guest. To the pupil's surprise, his teacher's visions were correct; a person was looking for their teacher indeed. Wang Shouren's new powers stunned other practitioners all around, and many even rumored that he had reached immortality.

一个不闻不语 3 年的僧人。

因筑室于会稽山阳明洞，王守仁自号“阳明子”，故世人又称他为“王阳明”。王阳明一直追求内心的平静，沉思了 2 年后，他想去过隐居的生活。但他放不下祖母和父亲。一日，他听闻杭州有一位不闻不语冥想了 3 年的僧人，便想前去一见。

To Be or Not to Be, a Monk.

For two arduous years in the Kuaiji Mountains, Wang Shouren practiced his meditations in a particular cave called the Yangming Cave. His experiences were so profound that he started to question whether he wanted to return home at all. He felt it was time to change his given name to something more enlightened.

The Chinese word “yang” means sun, and “ming” means light. Wang Shouren decided to name himself Wang Yangming, after the Yangming Cave, where he had so many significant meditation breakthroughs.

Wang Vangming had already accustomed himself to solitude living and contemplated his life as a monk. He thought monks might have the answers to more profound knowledge since many of them had dedicated much more time to meditations. However, becoming a monk would mean to leave all tangible connections behind, including family ties, which he found challenging. One day, he heard that an eminent monk from Hangzhou had been meditating in solitude for three years. He was so intrigued that he decided to pay a visit and learn more about his existence.

人性的启发。

找到那个和尚后，王阳明询问了他的家庭情况，和尚忍不住哭了起来。原来他沉默了 3 年，一直深深思念着自己的母亲。第二天，和尚就决定回家了。王阳明认为亲情是与生俱来无法割舍的，放弃亲人只顾自己的做法是不人道的。此时的王阳明似乎看到了意识的根源，即人性。

The Nature of a Human is the Root of Consciousness.

When Wang Yangming met the eminent monk, he was surprised at the gregarious nature of the man. They conversed into many deep subjects for many hours. When they got onto the topic of family, the monk began to cry, for it had been three years since he last saw his aging mother.

Wang Yangming empathized with the monk and discussed his views on the importance of the human heart. Unexpectedly, the monk felt suddenly enlightened by Wang Yangming's words. He decided to make a journey home the following day and return to his family.

Wang Yangming believed the relationship one has with their family is most meaningful, and those emotions should be cherished. It appeared to be against human nature to attain enlightenment by giving up one's family. After the meeting with the monk, he became profoundly aware that human consciousness came from recognizing human nature.

酒

34 岁，结识了一位挚友。

王阳明回到北京，结交了一位志同道合的朋友——湛若水。湛若水的师父陈白沙是明朝一位研究心学的大师。王阳明在与湛若水的交流中获得了重大启悟。

Gravitation Towards Xin Xue.

At age 34, Wang Yangming returned to Beijing for work, having left society for a significant amount of time; he felt quite lonesome. Luckily, he met a like-minded philosopher name Zhan Ruoshui, who was an esteemed pupil of a famous contemporary philosopher Chen Baisha. Chen Baisha was well known for laying the foundations of Xin Xue during the Ming Dynasty. Unlike Li Xue which focused on the outer; tangible, logical world, Xin Xue is another school of Confucian thought that focused on the study of the inner; intangible, emotional world. Wang Yangming gained a great deal of enlightenment from this friendship.

刘瑾乱政。

当时的朝廷内充满着各种对立势力，政权之争主要来自文官和宦官。其中有一位最腐败的宦官——刘瑾，他挪用大量公款，贪污了大量金银珠宝，还试图掌控皇帝。

Palace Life and Corruptions.

Wang Yangming returned to his work as an Imperial official. The palace was a complicated place with many politics within the ruling entities. At that time, there were opposing powers within the court, of which the conflict between civilian officials and eunuchs was the most intense. Liu Jin, a very powerful and corrupted eunuch of the time, had embezzled massive amounts of palace funds, gold, silver, and jewelry. He was steadily gaining power and devised an elaborate ploy to control the emperor. Many civilian officials who opposed him were thrown into prison.

35 岁，下诏狱。

王阳明为南京的言官们上疏，被刘瑾发现后，直接把他打入诏狱并廷杖了几十大板。因受不了这种刑罚而死去的官员不计其数，可以说，王阳明作为文官受到了当时最严厉的惩罚。

Indicted for Treason at Age 35.

Wang Yangming had always operated with a strong sense of justice. When he learned of Liu Jin’s ploys, he sent letters to the emperor, pleading for mercy for the wrongfully accused civilian officials. Liu Jin’s spies intercepted these letters and soon had Wang Yangming sentenced to prison for attempted treason. As an Imperial officer, he received the harshest punishment at the time: a public beating in the emperor’s court with wooden paddles. Most prisoners would die from such a penalty, but luckily Wang Yangming survived.

监禁的岁月。

王阳明在狱中正逢新年，此时，孤独、沮丧和恐惧环绕着他。

The Darkest Times.

Wang Yangming spent a challenging New Year in prison, feeling lonesome, depressed, and hopeless.

36 岁，死里逃生。

经历了牢狱之灾后，王阳明被刘瑾贬罚到中国西南地区的贵州龙场驿担任驿丞。在前往贵州的途中，刘瑾派刺客跟随王阳明，想要取他性命，但王阳明识破了他的计谋，写下绝命诗，脱下衣物，伪装成跳江现场。不仅刺客信以为真，而且绝大多数人，包括他的家人都以为他自杀了，甚至为他举行了葬礼。

Death at Age 36.

Wang Yangming survived his prison sentence despite the harsh conditions. Surprised by his will to live, Liu Jin had to release his prisoner. He ordered to have Wang Yangming sent to work in a rural posthouse in Longchang, Guizhou. Guizhou was a province in the far southwestern regions of China. To reach the posthouse from the capital, Wang Yangming had to be accompanied by two Imperial guards and walk the journey on foot. The foot guards were paid under the table and instructed to assassinate him during the long trip.

Wang Yangming had an intuition about the assassination plan and had been looking for opportunities to escape along the route. When they came upon a roaring river, he stripped naked and plunged into the river leaving his clothes and a suicide poem behind. The foot guards were surprised and swiftly returned to report his death. A funeral soon followed, which finally put Liu Jin at ease.

37 岁，龙场悟道。

王阳明还活着，他一直走了 4 个多月，终于在正德三年（1508）春抵达贵州龙场驿。他为自己做了一个石棺材，每晚睡在里面体验生死。在一个雷雨交加的夜里，他一身大汗地从石棺里醒来，一直困扰的问题突然解惑了。他顿悟了“圣人之道，吾性自足”的道理——必须求理于心，而非求理于外。王阳明的悟道是阳明心学的起点。

Reborn in Longchang.

Having survived the assassination attempt, Wang Yangming swam ashore and continued on his journey. In the spring of 1508, after an arduous four months-long trek on foot, he eventually arrived at Longchang posthouse. Locals thought he was a madman, for he built a stone coffin to sleep in every night and often contemplated death.

One stormy night, he suddenly had an epiphany—“The saint’s way was to become independent in one’s mind, and aware of the messages from within. One’s inner world was full of wisdom that the outer world could not teach.” Wang Yangming realized that the truth of one’s universe came from one’s inner heart, not from the physical world. Even he, who had lost all of his material possessions, status, title, and family ties, he still felt a powerful existence from deep within. In Longchang, he originated the “Yangming Xin Xue,” school of thought, and this later became a vital philosophy of the mind within the Confucianism body of studies.

价值之问。

他在陌生的部落人群中发现了自己的价值。他还创办了龙冈书院，教导当地人。一天，一位学生问道：“一朵花有价值吗？它的存在，又意味着什么呢？”王阳明说：“如果你关心这朵花，它就会对你产生影响。如果你不关心它，它就毫无价值。有的人可能嘴上说这朵花是美丽的，但如果他的内心不相信，那么这花对他而言也是没有价值的。”

What is Value?

Wang Yangming started to gain more self-awareness and consciousness as he contributed to the local tribes of the region. He built an academy called “Longgang College of Thought,” where he worked to enlighten the less-educated villagers. One day, one of his pupils asked, “Does a flower matter? Who is to say if this flower is beautiful or worth anything?” Wang Yangming answered, “The flower matters if you believe it matters. If you think it as no value, it must have no value. Some say it is beautiful and desirable. Some say it serves no purpose. What you believe is what matters.”

圣
心
理
满

圣贤之道。

王阳明认为既然人的本心囊括了世界万物之理（心即理），那么道德原理自然也存于人的本心，每个人都可成为圣贤。然而，在现实生活中，很多人的“本心”都被各种私欲所遮蔽了，所以无法看清道德原理。那么，要如何找回自己的“本心”呢？阳明先生的办法是：致良知。他相信“良知就是天理”，每个人都是有“良知”的，但要想成为圣贤，就要努力去除各种贪欲，在实际行动中实现“良知”。

Every Human can be Enlightened.

Wang Yangming believed that one's mind potentially embodied their unique truths of the universe; that conscience was a given principle of the heavens. He concluded that all humanity had the potential to reach higher levels of enlightenment and communication. However, human interactions seemed to be impeded by the need to create distinctions and discriminate between one conceptvs. another.

To show people how to achieve higher levels of enlightenment, Wang Yangming taught the locals his original theory—*The Theory of Innate Knowledge* or the concept of conscience. He urged people to find their inner sense of knowing and seek out their natural sense of goodness. "*One should work on self-awareness before interacting with others and refrain from negative emotions such as jealousy, greed, anger, and wrongful intentions. Most importantly, one should use their unique set of innate knowledge to guide them throughout their lives rather than search outwardly for answers.*"

理

38 岁，讲授心学。

王阳明在书院开展的心学讲授如火如荼，就连当时的贵州提学副使席书都前来听课。席书与王阳明见面时，问道：“您能告诉我朱熹和陆九渊的学问有什么异同吗？”王阳明回答说：“万物在没有得到我们内在的认可时，就等于不存在。我认为的不同之处对你而言是没有意义的，关键在于你认为的是什么。”席书还是感到困惑，与王阳明又讨论了 3 次后，终于大悟。两人最终也成为好朋友。

Spreading of Original Thinking.

Wang Yangming's original philosophies became very well known across the region. He gave regular lectures wherever he could. His concepts of Xin Xue became so popular that Xi Shu, the Deputy of National Education System, became fascinated by his teachings. One day, Xi Shu came to see Wang Yangming and asked, "There are two great Confucian writers, Zhu Xi, and Lu Jiuyuan, which one is better?" Wang Yangming replied, "Well, nothing makes sense without our inner contemplations. My answer to your question ultimately means nothing to you in the end; what you think is perhaps the most important." Left confused, Xi Shu continued to visit him three more times before finally understanding what he meant. The two had an enduring friendship years later.

知行合一。

王阳明在与席书讨论时提出了“知行合一”的思想。他认为世上有两种人：一种人是饱览群书，但只知纸上谈兵；另一种人则是冲动者，知之甚少、贸然行动，最后往往发现自己的努力都是徒劳的。所以王阳明相信 “知是行之始，行是知之成”。因此，为了充分理解生命和它所带来的体悟，人们必须先从概念上研究它，然后付诸行动。两种形式是一体的。

True Knowledge Through Awareness and Experience.

During the discussions with Xishu, Wang Yangming came upon the concept of “Zhi Xing He Yi,” the unity of awareness and experience to gain true knowledge. To grasp a full understanding of all things and events in life, one must first engage in awareness and then experience it.

He observed that there were two types of people in conventional society who had trouble gaining enlightenment and true knowledge. The first type was the academics, the armchair strategists; these were wellread educated individuals who lacked real-world practical experiences. They were full of theoretical concepts memorized through reading scriptures but had no experiential knowledge. The second type was the impatient emotion-driven people known for acting on raw impulses. They were poorly-read, short of theoretical expertise, and often found their ill-informed efforts in vain.

Wang Yangming observed that gaining initial awareness of concepts, intellectually primed one for the experience, and going through the experience then will result in gaining true knowledge of any matter. Therefore, to understand life to its fullness, awareness should never be divorced from experience.

圣

晋升与讲学。

朝廷传来宦官刘瑾下台的消息，于是王阳明在短时间内不断升职。回京之后，他与知己湛若水等人创办了一个讲坛。他的学生来自五湖四海，社会阶层多有不同，更有连地位和辈分都高于王阳明的人拜入其门下。

A New Beginning in the Capital.

Wang Yangming was doing well in his career when the news of the downfall of Liu Jin, the evil eunuch poured in. Wang Yangming felt it was finally safe to return to Beijing. When he returned, he and his longtime philosophical friend Zhan Ruoshui, started a public forum together.

Students from various backgrounds flocked in from all over the country. The forum became a place known to include some of the most renowned thinkers of the time.

39 岁，新的任职。

朝廷的任命也随之而来，他被任命为江西庐陵知县，主要调解辖区百姓的生活问题。上任以来，他勤政爱民，深受当地老百姓爱戴。他还劝谏当地人不要因为一时之怒与人争讼，要踏实务农、安居乐业。他告诉人们："'良知'这东西是每个人生来固有的，要在充分意识到自己本有'良知'的前提之下，通过实践把'良知'充分地体现出来。"

New Enlightenments Came with New Opportunities.

Wang Yangming continued to put his philosophies into practice, and through his excellent work, he became the Prefect of Luling County. All the previous prefects had left the position due to difficulties in communications with the locals. Wang Yangming's new duties were to mediate and resolve complaints between the people and the higher governance. His diligence and kindness earned him a reputable standing amongst the citizens. At the same time, Wang Yangming advertised extensively for the citizens to spend more time farming, bonding with their neighbors, and living in harmony with one another. He also encouraged citizens to engage in self-awareness practices and behave with their conscience.

41 岁，调往南京。

王阳明的心学开始变得非常流行，但因与传统教义的程朱理学背道而驰，引起了朝廷的关注。朝廷一面将他视为人才，一面又忌惮他的学说影响力太大，所以决定打发他去南京督管马政。

Relocation to Nanjing.

Many of Wang Yangming's original writings went against traditional Nee-Confucianism. New unfiltered ideas caught Imperial Governance's attention. The Imperial Court recognized him as a talent, yet feared the spanning influence of his teachings. The palace repositioned him to oversee the Imperial Stable of Nanjing, Jiangsu province. They believed sending Wang Yangming further south may minimize his intellectual impact over the Capital.

圣

淡泊名利，南下讲学。

他知道这是朝廷为了让他远离政治中心，但他本就淡泊名利，便乘势南下讲学。王阳明的教学风格不拘泥于常规，他有时在户外给学生授课， 有时又组织学生唱歌或诵读诗歌，很快吸引了大批学生。

New Location New Opportunities.

Instead of feeling frustrated to move again, Wang Yangming gladly took up the newly appointed position and saw it as an opportunity to spread his teachings to new regions. When he got to Nanjing, he continued to spread his ideologies. He often conducted his classes unconventionally, sometimes outside, and often with songs and poetry. His teaching style quickly gained popularity with the local Nanjing students.

45 岁， 新职任命。

45 岁的王阳明经举荐，当上了都察院左佥都御史，奉命巡抚南赣、汀漳等处（在今天的江西、福建等地区），其中南赣因“出产土匪”而闻名。一开始，王阳明以年岁大为由拒绝了高官厚禄，他打算回乡看望 90 多岁的祖母。但南赣匪患越来越严重，朝廷坚持让他上任。

New Promotion & Taking Care of Bandits.

At the age of 45, the Imperial Court promoted Wang Yangming to a very high position. The emperor appointed him as the head of the Investigative Bureau for a vast area spanning parts of today’s Jiangxi, Fujian, Hubei, and surrounding provinces. Of those areas, a place called Nangan was a known breeding ground for bandits, and Wang Yangming’s task was to minimize criminal activities in the region. Surprisingly, despite the hefty title and new impressive salary offered to him, Wang Yangming first declined the position. He wanted to stay close to home to take care of his aging grandmother. However, upon forceful insistence by the Imperial Palace, Wang Yangming had to relocate to his new position before the Nangan rampant bandit situation worsened.

46 岁，南赣剿匪，首先拿下詹师富。

南赣的土匪问题已猖獗长达 30 多年。王阳明实地调查，与当地人交谈收集情报后，总结出几个匪首的特点。多数将领都建议集中火力先攻打最强的一家，但王阳明做出了让人意想不到的决定——先拿下离得最远的詹师富，出其不意，攻其不备。詹师富节节败退，很快就被拿下。

The Four Rebel Warlords.

When Wang Yangming arrived in Nangan, four warlords ruled the region; Zhan Shifu, Lu Ke, Xie Zhishan, and Chi Zhongrong. The four rebels had reigned over the area for nearly three decades. Wang Yangming quickly went to work and spoke extensively with the locals to gauge the strengths and weaknesses of each warlord.

Other Imperial strategists advised Wang Yangming to start advancements on the strongest rebel army first. After careful considerations, he deemed it wisest to surprise attack the rebel residing furthest from town which was Zhan Shifu. As expected, the arrest came easy since the furthest warlord was caught entirely off guard.

卢柯投降。

随后王阳明写了一封招降信给卢珂，晓之以理，动之以情，劝他弃暗投明。卢柯被心理战术击溃，直接投降了。

Psychological Warfare.

Wang Yangming, then, wrote a warrant to Lu Ke and included a letter of compassion to reduce his sentencing if he agreed to surrender. Lu Ke, weak and intimidated by the news of Zhan Shifu's arrest, decided it was best to turn himself in with hopes for lighter sentencing.

谢志珊被判死刑。

第三个抓获的是相隔最近的谢志珊。王阳明十分欣赏聪明机智的谢志珊，但他觉得此人过于聪明而且野心勃勃，难以悔改。为了不铸成放虎归山之祸，王阳明将他判了死刑。

A Tiger will Remain a Tiger.

Two of the four warlords were caught and sentenced. Wang Yangming then went after Xie Zhishan, the third one who was known to be the most calculating and ambitious of them all. Wang Yangming recalled feeling great respect for the man of such abilities but recognized his insuppressible arrogance that could not be corrected. Xie Zhishan was given the death sentence at last.

"A ferocious tiger should not again be set free into the wild."

池仲容并非真心悔改。

最后剩下的是该地区实力最强大的匪徒池仲容。他的弱点是犹豫不决。王阳明写了一封招降信，告诉他，如果他愿意自首，判罚将大大减轻。池仲容放心不下，选了九十几名贴身护卫，一同去查探虚实。王阳明暗中观察池仲容的一举一动，看出他并非真心悔改。

Observing Human Nature.

There was one last warlord to arrest; Chi Zhongrong, who had the most active military force in the region. He was strong and intelligent. Indecisiveness was, however, his weakness. Wang Yangming drew up a letter, instructing him to confess to his crimes and surrender alone. In return, Wang Yangming will reduce his sentencing. Chi Zhongrong agreed, but did not follow the instructions and showed up to Wang Yangming's estate with several dozens of his bandit brothers. Wang Yangming saw the outcome as a breach of trust and had to devise a plan to get rid of the bandits taking over his home.

重获安宁。

新年快到了，王阳明一边在府里精心招待着土匪们，降低他们的心理防备，一边布下圈套。他告诉这位土匪老大，他为兄弟们准备了赏钱，但每次只能 5 人前来领取。等这 5 个人来拿赏钱之时，王阳明命人悄悄把他们杀掉。就这样，池仲容所有的贴身护卫全被分批解决了，池仲容也被斩首。这里终于重获了安宁。

Returning Peace to the People.

By this time Chi Zhongrong and his bandit brothers were holding up Wang Yangming's estate. Peaceful negotiations were no longer on the table. The Lunar New Year was fastly approaching, and Wang Yangming continued to entertain the bandits with excellent hospitality for them to drop their defenses.

On the Eve of the Lunar Year, Wang Yangming informed the bandits that he had prepared some generous gifts for everyone. He instructed the bandits to retrieve their gifts in groups of fives from the guest lobby. As the bandit groups arrived at the guest lobby, Wang Yangming's special forces were waiting to ambush them.

Group by group, Chi Zhongrong's bandit brothers were all gone, leaving the warlord alone and vulnerable in Wang Yangming's court. As the most influential warlord got beheaded, peace finally returned to the region.

1518年，修建濂溪书院。

为进一步广泛宣传王阳明的心学思想，他的门生记录和整理了他的语录，于正德十三年（1518）八月刻印《传习录》。九月，阳明先生组织修建濂溪书院，那里曾是理学鼻祖周敦颐（字濂溪）讲学之处。很快，四方学者都云集于此。

Rebirth of the Lianxi Academy in 1518.

In August 1518, *The Chuanxi Record* was published by one of Wang Yangming's star pupils to propagate Xin Xue concepts. This led to an excellent opportunity to renovate the Lianxi Academy, a place where ancient fathers of Neo-Confucianism gave lectures. Following the renovation, the Lianxi Academy became a renowned space for elite scholars and philosophy students.

王

48 岁，临危受命。

江西有变，一个酝酿了十年的反叛计谋即将上演。皇帝的叔公宁王朱宸濠蓄谋已久，计划发动一场大规模的政变来接管京城。王阳明又被派去掌控局势。那时王阳明的武装力量很有限，实在无法与拥兵 10 万的宁王抗衡。

A New Rebellion.

When Wang Yangming turned 48, he was called upon for yet another difficult task by the Imperial Palace. The emperor's uncle, Zhu Chenhao, also known as Lord Ning of Jiangxi Province, had planned a decade long coup d'etat to overthrow his emperor nephew. Wang Yangming was sent to capture Lord Ning and to cease the brewing rebellion. However, he was given a relatively limited military force against Lord Ning's strong army of 100,000 plus men.

分析局势。

王阳明分析局势：第一，宁王直攻毫无准备的北京，成功的机会最大；第二，宁王拿下南京，在南方自成一方霸主后，日后再与北京抗衡；第三，宁王优柔寡断，将同时错失夺取北京和南京的最佳时机，最终整个计划前功尽弃。

Military Calculations, Practicing Awareness First.

There were three possible outcomes of this coup d'etat. One, Lord Ning could easily win by steadily advancing his troops, as the palace was ill-prepared to defend itself. Two, Lord Ning's forces could seize Nanjing, which would give them an advantageous control over the southern regions of China. Ultimately, that would make attacking Beijing much easier down the line. Three, Lord Ning does not advance toward Beijing, nor does he seize Nanjing, and stays put. Then, Imperial Palace would have more time to draw up both defense and offense forces.

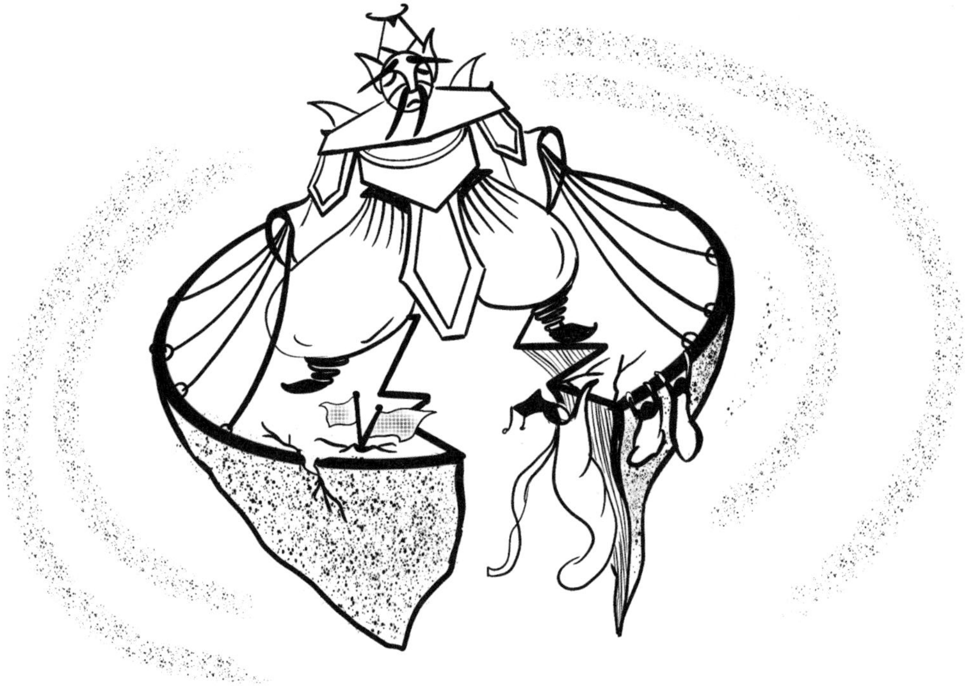

1519 年，智取南昌。

此时，为了将宁王留在南昌，迟滞他的进军时间，军力有限的王阳明伪造了朝廷军队将由各地进攻南昌的消息，并设法让宁王知悉。宁王中计，在南昌举棋不定，半个多月后，才如梦初醒，率领大部分军力攻向南京，南昌顿时防备空虚。王阳明当然不会错过这样的战机，率部直取南昌，并散布宁王已战败身亡的消息。南昌守军战意消沉，王阳明一鼓而定，拿下南昌。

Taking Nanchang with Limited Forces.

Wang Yangming's winning strategies would rest upon slowing Lord Ning's advancements, and so he decided to start with letter writing. Wang Yangming first forges an official document, stating that the Imperial Court had gathered massive numbers of troops and was en-route to attack Nanchang, the Capital of Jiangxi. Lord Ning intercepted the letters and decided to pull back his troops to protect his family within the Nanchang walls. Wang Yangming then bought plenty of time to deploy actual forces. Half a month later, Lord Ning arrived home and realized it was all a grand scheme to slow his tracks. He immediately gathered more forces, turns back to advance on Nanjing.

When Lord Ning left with more forces, Nanchang became poorly protected. Wang Yangming's troops then marched right into the Capital and propagated that Lord Ning had perished in battle. The whole city went into chaos and grief, and the sudden news paralyzed the defensive Capital guards. Wang Yangming was able to seize Nanchang with ease.

宁王被俘。

宁王还在继续征战，在得知南昌失守后，他开始犹豫了。他担心他的子民和家眷，开始制定撤退计划并派 2 万士兵火速返回南昌增援。王阳明神机妙算，只等宁王返回南昌，将他一举歼灭。宁王最终被俘，他的反叛计划宣告失败。

The Capture of Lord Ning.

Lord Ning was on his way to Nanjing when he received word about his hometown seized by the Imperial Army. He feared for his family and his people and decided to withdraw his troops once more in an attempt to take back Nanchang. As predicted, a psychologically defeated Lord Ning returned to Nanchang and was quickly captured by the Imperial Army.

圣

50 岁，“致良知”完整提出。

正德十六年（1521），王阳明开始揭示致良知的学说。经历了一系列的变乱后，王阳明更加相信良知，认为良知足以让人忘却遭受的患难，超脱生死，“致良知”三个字是圣人之门的核心所在。

Know Thy Conscience.

Wang Yangming coined the term “Know Thy Conscience,” and began to reveal his works and doctrines on the subject of morality. Wang Yangming believed in human’s ability to act with conscience, and that it was essential to seek out one’s inner sense of right or wrong and navigate the world accordingly.

50 岁，受封爵位。

正德皇帝朱厚照于正德十六年（1521）去世。新帝嘉靖皇帝朱厚熜登基后，王阳明因军功被封爵，爵号新建伯。

Crowned Earl at Age 50.

In 1521, emperor Zhu Houzhao died. The newly crowned emperor Zhu Houcong ascended to the throne, and immediately awarded Wang Yangming for his lifelong service of excellence for state affairs, granting him the prestigious title of “The Earl of Xinjian.”

奠

51岁，父亲去世。

嘉靖元年（1522），王阳明的父亲去世。曾高中状元的父亲，是一位睿智、通晓事理的智者。他提醒王阳明，月满则亏，晋升和好运也可能会伴随着不幸和不确定性，所以无论如何一定要为那些突如其来的变化做好心理准备。

Death in the Family,1522.

Wang Yangming’s father, a respected former Imperial examination scorer, passed away in 1522. He was a strong-willed father of great wisdom, and on his deathbed, he reminded his son that the moon begins to wane the moment it becomes full. For Wang Yangming, it meant that the new Imperial promotion could very likely to be followed by uncertainties.

心学受打压。

新帝认可王阳明的成就，但同时也禁遏了王阳明的心学。充满嫉妒、渴望权力和雄心勃勃的官员们开始抵制心学的传播，朝廷也不支持心学，因为新思想不利于思想的统一。

Banning of Xin Xue Philosophy.

The Imperial Palace recognized Wang Yangming as a man of great war strategies, not a philosopher. As the Earl, Wang Yangming met a lot of adversities from jealous Court officials, and they tried to stagnate his philosophical work, deeming them a threat to the unity of the nation. The Imperial Court decided to demote his Xin Xue concepts and did not wish him to continue with the propagation work.

圣
圣

多次请辞。

王阳明多次提出辞去职位，都没有得到同意。此时，王阳明继续在家乡讲学，并逐渐完善了他的心学思想。

Finishing his Thoughts in Secret.

Unable to publically continue with his Xin Xue philosophical work, Wang Yangming felt his high title was stifling his life's purpose as an enlightened philosopher. He repeatedly pleaded with the Emperor to withdraw from his position but was denied. During this time, he continued to give lectures in his hometown and proceeded to finish his philosophical writings in secret.

圣命难违。

1527 年，朝廷镇压不了广西地区的土司叛乱，又命王阳明出山。起初，王阳明考虑到自己当时的身体越来越差，并不想答应。但朝廷旨意已下，圣命难违。

The Last Rebellion.

In 1527, a new rebellion surfaced in Guangxi, located in the southern region of China. Wang Yangming was again sent to strategize and work on peace negotiations. Considering his declining health conditions , Wang Yangming initially refused the commission. However, all beings under the Mandate of Heaven were obliged to execute direct orders from the Emperor, and Wang Yangming was no exception.

天泉证道。

出发前，王阳明依然不忘讲学。一天晚上，他在天泉桥上与两个学生一起探讨心学，在离开之际，留下了四句心学宗旨。这次谈话后来被称为“天泉证道”。

Tianquan Path of Righteousness.

On the last night upon departure for his new mission, he held a private meeting with two of his disciples on the Tianquan Bridge. Wang Yangming left his pupils with four key philosophies, which were then later recorded as the *Tianquan Zheng Dao – The Tianquan Path of Righteousness.*

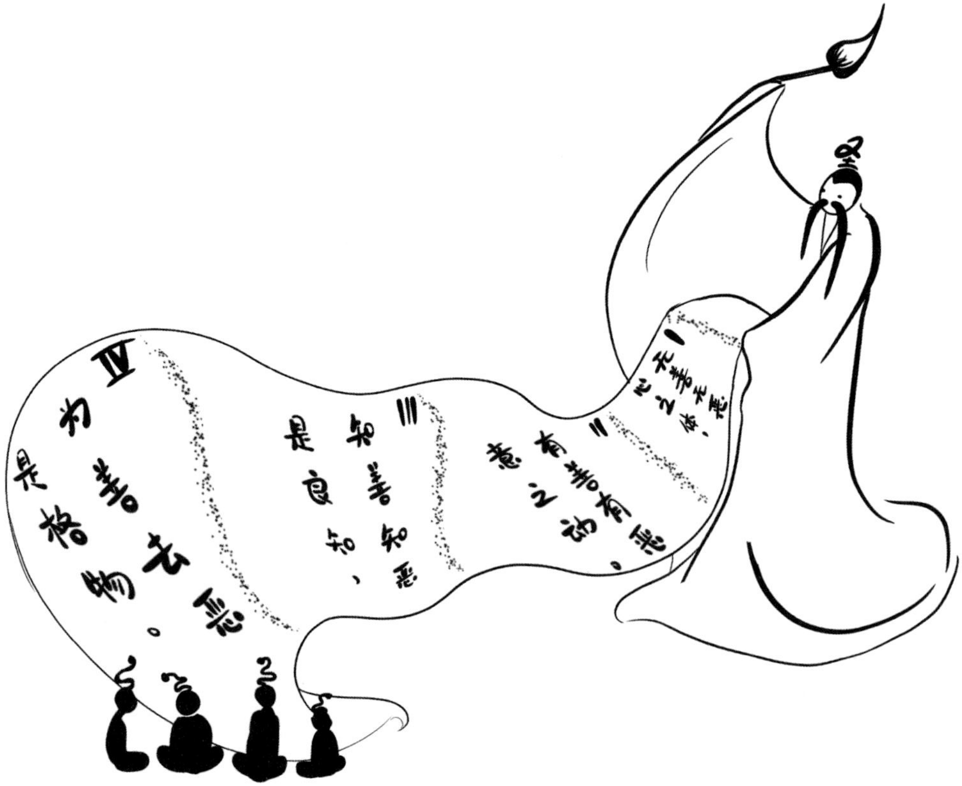
Ⅰ 无善无恶心之体、
Ⅱ 有善有恶意之动。
Ⅲ 知善知恶、是良知
Ⅳ 为善去恶是格物。

心学宗旨。

无善无恶心之体，
有善有恶意之动。
知善知恶是良知，
为善去恶是格物。

The Four Pillars of Xin Xue.

Virtue and evil do not exist in the world,
Virtue or evil depends on a human's intentions.
The ability to tell virtue from evil is an innate human ability,
It is human to do good rather than evil.

1528 年，再一次胜利。

为了平定叛乱，王阳明写了封招降信给叛乱头目卢苏和王受，劝说头目如果投降就免除他们的罪行。三人见面后，王阳明才知道他们并不是真正意义上的叛匪，问题的根源来自断藤峡和八寨的这群土司。卢苏和王受为报答王阳明的明断，带兵与王阳明合力破敌，一举歼灭了土匪的老巢。

A Champion of Truth and Justice.

When Wang Yangming arrived in Guangxi, the locals led him to two rebellious bandit leaders, Lu Su, and Wang Shau. Wang Yangming, as usual, started with mediation letters asking the two for confessions to lighten their sentencing. The rebels came peacefully, and after some negotiations, Wang Yangming realized they weren't criminals. The threat, instead, came from warlords who were active in neighboring regions Duanteng Xia and Ba Zhai. The two bandits negotiated their sentencing and offered to assist Wang Yangming's forces to capture the true leaders of the rebellion. Finally, with the help of Lu Su and Wang Shau, the Imperial troops returned victoriously, and the uprising was pacified.

57 岁，功成身退。

消息传回宫中，竟然有人上书弹劾王阳明，说他未经朝廷许可，擅自进剿。此时，王阳明身体状况每况愈下，便上书朝廷，告老还乡。他早已看淡荣辱得失，决定义无反顾踏上回家之路。

An Unconventional Win Resulted in Demotion.

Guangxi Province became peaceful again, and good news found its way into the Imperial Palace as well as the unconventional methods Wang Yangming deployed. The Imperial Court was not pleased with his direct disobedience of the prime directive. The court wanted to impeach him for using Imperial forces to suppress the unwarranted warlords. Wang Yangming’s health was in steady decline, and he cared little for the Imperial opinions of him. He felt he was near death and pleaded with the Emperor to resign from office so he could return home to his family. This time the Emperor agreed.

光明的一生。

王阳明从广西乘船归乡，途中经过伏波将军庙。他回想起那正是他 15 岁时梦见的东汉伏波将军马援。看着大殿里供奉的马援将军，就好似美梦成真。告别了伏波将军庙，船只继续朝着余姚老家慢慢前进，此时王阳明的身体已经非常虚弱。1529 年 1 月 9 日，王阳明在南安府（今江西大余县）青龙铺江面的船上，留下此生最后一句话：“此心光明，亦复何言。”

The End of the Enlightened Path.

The Emperor allowed Wang Yangming to return home directly from Guangxi. On his way back in an Imperial boat, he noticed a grand temple built in the memory of an ancient general Fubo Mayuan, a great iconic warrior. Wang Yangming stopped the vessel and struggled into the temple with his frail body. He was amazed to find out the figure was the same as his childhood dreams, and it was his last magnificent glance. On January 9th. 1529, Sir Wang Yangming passed away in his Imperial boat crossing the Qinglongpu River of the Nan'an Prefecture. Still, hundreds of miles from his hometown, his last words upon death were: “I have lived the life of light, and all is enough.”

红旗出版社
HONGQI PRESS
推动进步的力量

图书在版编目（CIP）数据

你好！王阳明 /（美）李玉琼绘；李谷鸣，（美）李玉琼著. -- 北京：红旗出版社，2020.1
ISBN 978-7-5051-4979-3

Ⅰ. ①你… Ⅱ. ①李… ②李… Ⅲ. ①王守仁（1472–1528）–生平事迹–少儿读物 Ⅳ. ① B248.2–49

中国版本图书馆 CIP 数据核字 (2019) 第 245438 号

书　　名　你好！王阳明
作　　者　（美）李玉琼 绘；李谷鸣，（美）李玉琼 著

出 品 人　唐中祥　　　　责任校对　曾晓蓉
总 监 制　褚定华　　　　英文校对　徐　珊
特邀编审　吴　光　希　言　　责任印务　金　硕
责任编辑　徐　澜　周婷婷　　封面设计　顾　页

出版发行　红旗出版社
地　　址　（南方中心）杭州市体育场路 178 号
邮　　编　310039　　　　编 辑 部　0571-85310271
E-mail　1793516722@qq.com　　发 行 部　（北京）010-57270296
（杭州）0571-85311330
欢迎项目合作　项目电话　（北京）010-57274627
（杭州）0571-85310806
图文排版　杭州美虹电脑设计有限公司
印　　刷　杭州富春电子印务有限公司

开　　本　889 毫米 ×1194 毫米　1/24
字　　数　100千字　　印　　张　$5\frac{1}{3}$
版　　次　2020 年1月北京第1 版　2020 年5月杭州第2 次印刷

书　　号　ISBN 978-7-5051-4979-3　定　　价　39.80 元